D1628000

Emerald Publishing

CONDUCTING YOUR OWN COURT CASE

Revised edition

HELEN LITLE

Emerald Publishing
www.emeraldpublishing.co.uk

Emerald Publishing
Brighton BN2 4EG

© Straightforward Publishing 2008

ISBN
ISBN 13: 9781847160 88 1

Printed and bound by Biddles Ltd Kings Lynn Norfolk.

Cover design by Bookworks Islington

CONTENTS

INTRODUCTION

Without doubt, the legal system is complex and daunting and most people who go to court to either resolve disputes or to defend themselves when sued, will use a solicitor or barrister. Such professionals do not come cheaply. This fact, above all, can influence a person's decision whether or not to go to court.

More and more people are choosing to go down the route of Do-it-yourself representation. These people are known as litigants-in-person. More and more courts are sympathetic to self-representation and judges will often help the litigant. This book attempts to throw light on the whole legal process by adopting a specific approach towards explaining the processes involved. Chapter 1 deals with an outline of how the system works and who is who within the various courts. The purpose is to provide a backdrop which should prove invaluable to the litigant. Chapter 2 explains the role more fully of solicitors and barristers and also points to other sources of legal help available. Chapter 3 outlines the importance of finding a solution to problems before they get to court, as this avoids an often long and costly battle. Chapters 4 to 6 outline the processes within the various courts and puts forward case studies which should help the litigant in person gain an idea of the processes involved.

Overall, this brief but invaluable guide to conducting your own court case, presented through building blocks to the actual presentation of a case, should prove an indispensable aid to representing yourself in court.

1

HOW THE LEGAL SYSTEM WORKS.

Before deciding to embark upon legal action, whether you are doing so without the aid of a solicitor, or with a solicitor, it is essential to understand the workings of the British legal system. Only then can you begin to conduct a case or to understand how to get the most out of the system.

Legal terms explained
There is a detailed glossary of terms at the back of this book which deals with commonly used legal jargon. However, it is useful to highlight the most common terms right at the outset, as they will be used frequently throughout the book:

Claimant – when legal proceedings are brought, the person or persons, or organisation, bringing the case is called the claimant.

Defendant – The individual or organisation being sued, and therefore defending, is called the defendant.

Solicitor – a solicitor is the lawyer you will (or might) see for legal advice relating to your case. This person will have undertaken many years of study and passed all the necessary legal examinations. We will be discussing solicitors in more depth a little later.

Barrister – A Barrister is a lawyer who is a specialist in what is known as advocacy, i.e. speaking in court. A Barrister will have been called to the bar by one of the Inns of Court and passed the barristers professional examinations. A solicitor will instruct a barrister to represent you in court proceedings. However, barristers will not normally be the persons giving individuals legal advice in the first instance. The legal profession is, basically, split into two, barristers and solicitors, both of whom are lawyers.

Writ – A judicial writ is issued to bring legal proceedings. Civil cases are started in the courts by issuing and serving a writ. This document is completed either by an individual bringing the case or by a solicitor on behalf of the individual. It is issued by the court.

Litigant in person – a litigant is someone who is bringing legal proceedings or suing. A litigant-in-person is someone who chooses to represent themselves in court, without a lawyer.

Damages – Civil claims in the courts are for damages, which is money claimed from the defendant to compensate the claimant for loss arising from the action of default of the defendant. An example might be the sale of a good that has caused injury to a person and it is alleged that the good was faulty at the time of purchase.

Using the legal system to resolve disputes

If you are contemplating any form of legal action, with or without solicitors, it is necessary to have a basic idea of how the system works. The more that you understand the processes underlying the legal system, the more effective you will be, both as a citizen and as a potential litigant.

The structure of the court system

The court system in the United Kingdom deals, in the main, with civil and criminal cases. They are heard in either the county court (civil cases) and the Magistrates and Crown Courts (criminal cases)

Civil cases are those that typically involve breaches of contract, personal injury claims, divorce cases, bankruptcy hearings, debt problems, some employment cases, landlord and tenant disputes and other consumer disputes, such as faulty goods. These are the cases that are most often dealt with by the individual acting as litigant in person.

Criminal cases are those such as offences against the person, theft, damage to property, murder and fraud. These cases, if of a non-serious nature, are heard in the magistrate's courts. If of a serious nature, then they will be heard in the Crown Court and tried by jury. Although individuals do represent themselves in the Crown Court it is more usual to use a solicitor in these cases.

Criminal cases

The more serious criminal cases are tried on the basis of a document called the *indictment.* The defendant is indicted on criminal charges specified in the indictment by the prosecutor. In most cases, the prosecution is on behalf of the Crown (State) and is handled by an official agency called the Crown Prosecution Service, which takes the case over from the police who have already investigated most of the evidence. The first stage will be to decide whether there is a case to answer. This process, called committal, will be dealt with by a magistrate on the basis of evidence disclosed in papers provided by the prosecutor. If the case proceeds, it is heard in the Crown Court. There are about 70 Branches of the Crown Court in the United Kingdom. Addresses can be obtained from the Court service website: www.courtservice.uk The trial is before a judge and jury. The judge presides over the trial and considers legal issues. The jury will decide on the facts (who is telling the truth) and applies the law to those facts. In criminal cases, the prosecution has to prove, beyond reasonable doubt, that the defendant is guilty. The defendant does not have to prove innocence. However, it is the jury who will observe the prosecutor and defending lawyer and decide the case.

In less serious criminal cases (which comprise over 90% of criminal cases) the case is sent for summary and trial in one of over 400 *magistrates* courts, addresses again from the court service website. A summary trial means that there is no committal or jury. The case is decided by a bench of magistrates. In most cases there are three magistrates who are lay (unqualified) persons but are from the local community. However, there are now an increasing number of 'stipendiary' magistrates, paid magistrates who are qualified lawyers.

Those defendants in criminal cases who are dissatisfied with verdicts may be able to appeal, as follows:

- from the Magistrates courts there is an appeal to the Crown Court on matters of fact or law.
- From the Crown Court, it might be possible to appeal to the Criminal Division of the court of Appeal on matters of fact or law.
- Certain legal disputes arising in the Magistrates court or the Crown Court can be taken before the divisional court of the High Court.
- Matters of important legal dispute arising in the Crown Court can be taken to the House of Lords

Civil cases

The majority of people who buy this book will be taking civil action of one form or another. Increasingly, people are becoming litigants-in-person as this enables people to access the courts and obtain justice without incurring high costs. The only real costs are the court fees and other incidental costs such as taking time off work and so on.

The county court

The county court deals with civil cases, which are dealt with by a judge, or a district judge. A case can be started in any county court but can be transferred back to the defendant's local court.

All cases arising from regulated credit agreements must be started in the county court, whatever their value.

County courts deal with a wide range of cases ranging from bankruptcy and family matters to landlord and tenant disputes. The most common cases are:

- Consumer disputes, for example faulty goods or services
- Personal injury claims, caused by negligence, for example traffic accidents, accidents caused by faulty pavements and roads, potholes etc
- Debt problems, for example someone seeking payment
- Some undefended divorce cases and some domestic violence cases
- Race and sex discrimination cases
- Employment problems, usually involving pay.

Small claims in the county court

A case in the county court, if it is defended, is dealt with in one of three ways. These ways are called 'tracks' The court will, when considering a case, decide which procedure to apply and allocate the case to one of the following tracks:

- The small claims track
- The fast track
- The multi-track

The small claims track is the most commonly used and is the track for claims of £5000 or less. Overall, the procedure in the small claims track is simpler than the other tracks and costs are not usually paid by the losing party.

Following a brief summary of the other courts in the United Kingdom, we will be looking in more detail, in chapter 4, at how to commence and process a small claim. In the main, readers of this book will be concerned with the small claims track and it is therefore necessary to outline that process in depth. We will also be looking, in chapter 2, at the legal help scheme. This scheme enables those with a low income to get free legal advice from a solicitor and assistance with preparing a case.

The magistrates' court

As we have seen, magistrate's courts deal with criminal cases in the first instance and also deal with some civil cases. The cases are heard by Justices of the Peace or by District Judges (magistrates courts). All cases heard in a magistrate's court are from within their own area.

Criminal offences in the magistrate's court

Magistrate's courts deal with criminal offences where the defendant is not entitled to a trial by jury. These are known as 'summary offences' and involve a maximum penalty of six months imprisonment and/or a fine up to £5000. Magistrates also deal with offences where the defendant can choose trial by jury. If this is the case, the case is passed up to the Crown Court.

The youth court

The youth court deals with young people who have committed criminal offences, and who are aged between 10-17. The youth court is a part of the magistrate's court and up to three specially trained magistrates hear the case.

If a young person is charged with a very serious offence, which in the case of an adult is punishable by 14 years imprisonment or more, the youth court can commit him/her for trial at the Crown Court.

Civil cases in the magistrates' court

As we have seen, the vast majority of civil cases are dealt with in the county courts. However, the magistrate's court can deal with a limited number of cases, as follows:

- Some civil debts, e.g. arrears of income tax, national insurance contributions, council tax and Value added Tax arrears
- Licences, for example, licences for clubs and pubs
- Some matrimonial problems, e.g. maintenance payments and removing a spouse from the matrimonial home

- Welfare of children, e.g. local authority care orders or supervision orders, adoption proceedings and residence orders

The Crown Court

The more serious criminal cases are tried in the Crown Court. The following are dealt with:

- Serious criminal offences to be heard by judge and jury
- Appeals from the magistrates court-which are dealt with by a judge and at least two magistrates
- Someone convicted in the magistrates court may be referred to the Crown Court for sentencing.

The High Court

The High Court will hear appeals in criminal cases and will also deal with certain civil cases. The High Court also has the legal power to review the actions or activities of individuals and organisations to make sure that they are both operating within the law and also are acting justly. The High Court consists of three divisions, as follows:

The Family Division

The Family Division of the High Court will deal with more complex defended divorce cases, wardship, adoption, domestic violence and other cases. It will also deal with appeals from the magistrates and county courts in matrimonial cases.

The Queens Bench Division

The Queens Bench Division of the High Court will deal with larger claims for compensation, and also more complex cases for compensation. A limited number of appeals from county and magistrates courts are also dealt with. The Queens Bench Division can also review the actions of individuals or organisations and hear libel and slander cases.

The Chancery Division

The Chancery Division deals with trusts, contested wills, winding up companies, bankruptcy, mortgages, charities, and contested revenue such as income tax.

The Court of Appeal

The Court of Appeal deals with civil and criminal appeals. Civil appeals from the high and county courts are heard, as well as from the Employment Appeals Tribunal and the Lands Tribunal. Criminal Appeals include appeals against convictions in the Crown Courts, and points of law referred by the Attorney General following acquittal in the Crown Court or where a sentence imposed is seen as too lenient.

The House of Lords

The House of Lords deals mostly with appeals from the Court of Appeal, where the case involves a point of law of public importance. Appeals are mostly about civil cases although the Lords do deal with some criminal appeals. If there is dissatisfaction with a finding of the House of Lords then the claimant can take a case higher through the European Court System.

The Court of First Instance

The Court of First Instance is based in Luxembourg. A case can be taken to this court if European Community law has not been implemented properly by a national government or there is confusion over its interpretation or it has been ignored. A case which is lost in the Court of First Instance may be taken to appeal to the European Court of Justice.

The European Court of Justice of the European Communities

The European Court of Justice advises on interpretation of European Community law and takes action against infringements. It examines whether the actions of those members of the European Community are valid and clarifies European Community law by making preliminary rulings. It also hears appeals against decisions made by the Court of First Instance.

The European Court of Human Rights

The European Court of Human Rights deals with cases in which a person thinks that their human rights have been contravened and for which there is no legal remedy within the national legal system.

2

LEGAL HELP

For those contemplating taking legal action, there are a number of options. The first option is usually to visit a solicitor to gain legal help and to launch your case. However, it is a fact that many people are put off going to see a solicitor because of the costs involved. In many cases, unfortunately, this results in people being denied justice. This book is designed to ensure that those who wish to pursue their own case without the help of a solicitor can do so. Nevertheless, it is very useful indeed to understand what it is exactly that solicitors and barristers do and what their role is within the legal system and to also understand what other forms of legal help are available.

As we have seen, the costs of launching a civil case in the county court are minimal and the process is relatively straightforward. Chapter 4 deals with this process in depth. However, many people would still rather work with the help and guidance of a solicitor. This chapter outlines the work of solicitors, the other forms of legal advice available and also outlines the legal help scheme for those on low income.

Solicitors
Solicitors are trained to deal with a large range of legal problems. Large firms tend to be formed as partnerships and will have

specialist solicitors working in defined areas, such as crime, family, landlord and tenant and so on. Solicitors are heavily regulated by the Law society and must have no personal interest in the matter in dispute. Solicitors must take out compulsory indemnity insurance to indemnify them against negligence and the profession also runs a 'compensation' fund to compensate those who have suffered loss at the hands of unscrupulous solicitors.

Solicitors do not come cheap and will charge by the hour, charges being anything up to £90 per hour. There are often fixed fees for matters such as conveyancing.

For advice which they consider they may need a second opinion, solicitors will usually seek 'counsels advice' which is given by a barrister. A Barrister is a specialist in advocacy, operating from 'chambers' and costing anything up to £300 per hour. Often, high profile cases, such as tax evasion and libel and slander, will be conducted by barristers.

Anyone considering launching legal action will need to consider whether or not they wish to use a solicitor. For simple small claims, it is not necessary to use a solicitor as the process is designed to assist the layperson. However, the following instances may demand that you use a solicitor:

- Moving house

- Getting divorced (depending on the complexity of the divorce-many straightforward divorced are carried out in person)
- Getting arrested
- Other complex legal maters, such as negligence and nuisance compensation claims

Never use a solicitor without first obtaining an estimate of their likely charges in the matter. Some solicitors will attempt to be vague over such matters but it is highly desirable for you to be assertive on the matters of cost estimates. Ensure that the estimate is in writing and is broken down and clear. Most solicitors now issue a 'client engagement' letter to their clients as recommended by the Law Society.

Solicitor's charges will principally be based on the amount of time spent on the case, as solicitors usually charge by the hour. The longer it takes, the more it will cost you. If the matter is complex, a solicitor will usually look at the case and decide how much they will do and how much a junior will cover, in order to minimise the costs.

The notion 'the cheapest is best' is not always correct or advisable when dealing with solicitors, as the quality of advice and degree of organisation will vary according to the solicitors used. Usually, larger practices are better able to offer specialist advice and are also better organised and easier to get access to.

Choosing the right firm

The best way to choose a solicitor is by recommendation, for example one that a friend has used. It will be necessary to ensure that the firm that is recommended has the right experience to represent you adequately.

In some areas, all solicitors will generally have a specialism, such as property conveyancing. However, for obtaining compensation for personal injury, or an employment law dispute then you will need to ensure that a firm of solicitors has this expertise.

Using a solicitor

Solicitors are, generally, very thorough and meticulous. They have to be, given the professional standards and codes that they have to deal with and also because of the need to obtain all the facts. It is important that, in the first instance, you give the solicitor as much clear information as possible. Further ongoing contact by telephone is charged for. Most solicitors will monitor calls carefully and enter these in a log or journal. Time is money, so therefore you should ensure:

- All information is passed on at the beginning
- Do not contact the solicitor too often. Ask for regular progress reports to be sent to you
- Respond to requests for information from the solicitor straight away
- Require an initial estimate and notification when costs reach the level of the estimate

Aim for a friendly, professional and open working relationship with a solicitor as you are both striving towards the same goal, that is to win your case.

Finally, if you search on line then you can access a wide range of solicitors and gain an indication of their specialist areas. A word of caution: you should always be wary of those solicitors who advertise on television. Many will say 'no win no fee'. Although this sounds attractive, the fees if you do win can be very high indeed. If you do intend to use such a firm make sure that you understand the charges at the outset.

In some cases, you may be dissatisfied with a solicitor and will wish to complain or even sue. If this is the case then contact the Office for the Supervision of Solicitors or the Legal Services Ombudsman (addresses at the back of this book).

Other sources of legal advice

There is no legal requirement to use a solicitor. People do so when they feel that they need advice in the first instance or feel that their case may be too complex. However, there are law centres operating in each local authority area, often offering free advice and specialising in family and community matters, such as health and housing. Citizens Advice Bureau also offer advice and can be found in each area. In addition, the CAB has on line advice which can be accessed through their web site. Enter www. Citizen's advice and the site will appear. This is very useful and has written advice on a wide range of areas.

Some bodies, such as the consumer association, also offer advice, again either by phone or on line, about a range of issues affecting the consumer. In addition, if you are a member of a trade union you may be able to get free legal advice from this source, Some banks offer free legal advice and it is worthwhile giving your local branch a ring.

Legal aid

Legal aid can be accessed via the 'legal help scheme'. This scheme used to be known as the 'Green Form' scheme but has changed its name and emphasis.

The legal help scheme provides access to free legal advice for people with low incomes. The solicitor or organisation offering this help has to have a contract with the Legal Services Commission to be able to provide assistance.

What does the scheme cover

The legal help scheme covers help from a solicitor including general legal advice and writing letters, negotiating, getting a barristers opinion and preparing a written case for a tribunal. The scheme does not provide for being represented by a solicitor in court (although the *help at court scheme* and *controlled legal representation* scheme might. The solicitor that you are dealing with will give you further advice concerning these schemes.

The scheme may also cover the costs of mediation. Mediation is a process of negotiation where the parties are helped by a neutral mediator who will assist them to find a mutually acceptable solution.

Legal problems covered by the scheme

The legal advice scheme will provide advice on general legal problems, including the following areas:

- undefended divorce, maintenance or disputes over children
- Conveyancing necessary to carry out a court order or following a divorce settlement or legal separation
- Contested adoptions
- Preparing for tribunals, for example, unfair dismissal or unified appeal tribunals (benefit appeals)
- Making a will if someone is over 70 or disabled, or is a parent making provision for a disabled child or is a single parent appointing a guardian
- Accident claims – advice, preparing a case for criminal injuries compensation, getting medical reports.

For the case to qualify for the legal help scheme, two criteria must be met:

- Help may be provided only where it is shown there is a benefit to the person
- Help may be provided only if it is shown that it is reasonable for the matter to be funded.

The legal help scheme covers two hours worth of work by a solicitor (three in the case of divorce or judicial separation). The solicitor can apply for extra time to finish the work under the scheme. In addition to these criteria, there may be other criteria applied, depending on the nature of the case.

Financial conditions for the scheme

If a person has capital over £8000, (£3000 for immigration cases), that person will not be eligible for help under the scheme. This limit is for a person with no dependants.

Income

If a person is claiming income support or income based job seekers allowance, that person will be deemed to be within the limits for the scheme. If this is not the case, eligibility will depend on disposable income. If a person is receiving working families tax credit or disabled persons tax credit then that person may be eligible for assistance depending on the amount of benefit received.

When assessing a person's disposable income, which is income after all expenses, then allowances will be made for dependants. If a person's disposable income is £649 per month or more (2006/7) then that person will not get free legal help.

Extra costs that the person may have to pay

If a person is awarded property or money as a result of advice under the scheme in a family case, the solicitor's costs may be taken from the amount.

The amount taken will vary. In some cases where it is seen that hardship will result then no costs are taken. It is important to ensure that this is made clear at the outset and you know what the position is. The website of the Legal Services Commission www.legalservicescommission.gov.uk has a download which deals in-depth with the financial aspects of legal help.

How to apply

If a person qualifies for the legal help scheme, they need to see a solicitor or organisation with a contract to provide legal help under the scheme. The solicitor will ask the person to fill in an application form at the initial interview. The solicitor will then be able to decide whether the person qualifies.

3

SOLVING DISPUTES BEFORE TAKING LEGAL ACTION

If you are in dispute and feel that you need to revert to using the law, before you do so you should try to solve the dispute amicably. You need to establish the facts of the matter and examine whether or not there actually is a dispute at all or whether the problem could be solved without recourse to the law. You also need to look at the dispute in terms of whether or not realistically you are going to win or whether you will be involved in a long and drawn out expensive battle that you are unlikely to win.

You should ask yourself the following questions before committing a case to court:

- Is your case clear cut or does your opponent have a clear argument?
- What do others think about your case? You need to ask someone who is unbiased.
- What is the value of your claim/ Does it justify the time and expense of going to court?
- What are the likely solicitors (if any at any point) costs?

Payments into court

If you do go to court, it is worth noting that the defendant can pay a sum into court, representing the amount of money for which the defendant would settle. If the case proceeds and the plaintiff wins less than that sum, then the defendant will not have to pay the plaintiffs costs. You should always think carefully about accepting a payment into court and should take legal advice.

Timing of court action

Court actions can, by their very nature, be slow and painstaking. However, the timing depends very much on the nature of the dispute. In cases of emergency where an order is needed to prevent someone from doing something this can be made in a matter of hours. These are known as 'injunctions'. Most disputes, however, often take many months to go through the court procedure. So do not expect a quick victory, as the wheels of justice turn at their own pace.

Damages

Damages is the money which is won in compensation from the defendant. The judge in the dispute will make the order as to damages, which normally consists of a sum of money necessary to place the claimant in the same position as he or she was before the incident occurred. There is an obligation to 'mitigate' loss which means that the claimant should take reasonable care to reduce the loss as much as possible. Damages can be reduced where the claimant is at fault, for example where the claimant has added to the injury suffered by his or her own actions at the time and subsequently.

Damages for criminal injury

In cases where a criminal injury has occurred and compensation cannot be obtained from the perpetrator, you may be able to get compensation from the Criminal Injuries Compensation Authority. The CICA gives out compensation amounting to millions of pounds each year. The address of the Authority is found at the rear of this book.

The eligibility requirements of the programme are that the matter must be reported to police as soon as possible after it has occurred. The matter has to be filed to the CICA within two years. Those who can claim are:

- Victims of crime
- Dependants of homicide victims
- Foreign citizens

Procedures

A claimant can obtain an application from CICA, local victim support schemes, Crown Court witness service, local police stations or local citizens advice bureau. The application should be sent to CICA. The authorities initial decision should be made within 12 months, while reviews and hearings can take several months longer. Compensation can be paid as soon as CICA is notified that the claimant accepts the decision.

Benefits and award limits
The maximum award is £500,000.

Compensable costs
- Medical expenses
- Mental Health expenses
- Lost wages for disabled victims
- Lost support for dependants of homicide victims
- Funerals
- Travel
- Rehabilitation for disabled victims
- Pain and suffering
- Bereavement
- Loss of parental services

Emergency awards
Interim payments can be made where a final decision as to the appropriate award is uncertain. For example, where the victim's medical prognosis is unclear.

Funding
The programme is funded by the taxpayer

Appealing against a CICA decision
There is an appeals panel, which will hear appeals against the findings of the CICA. Details can be obtained from the headquarters of CICA.

What to do if you are sued.

In addition to deciding to sue someone, you may find yourself in receipt of a summons or writ through the post. The summons or writ will always provide for a written defence, which has to be filed within a time periods clearly outlined on the document. If you do not file the defence then a judgement will be entered against you automatically.

When receiving a writ or summons the following actions should be taken:

- Check to whom the document is addressed. It may be that it should be for someone else. If this is the case forward it on or return to the sender
- If it is for you read it very carefully indeed. With the summons will be a particulars of claim which will outline what the case is against you
- Note any time limits that you have to adhere to

What form of action you should take will very much depend on the nature of the writ or summons. As we discussed, the case will either be civil or criminal. Most people are aware of the basic criminal offences, such as driving offences etc. A small claim against you could be for a variety of actions, such as breach of contract or negligence.

Most criminal offences require attendance at court. Minor criminal offences require attendance at the magistrate's court. Civil offences will require attendance at County Court if you decide to defend. If you admit a claim then the matter can be settled by post.

In criminal offences, the judge will pass sentence. In civil cases, the judge will enter a judgement and decide on a level of compensation relevant to the action.

If the defendant does not pay the money arising from the judgement, then the following remedies are available:

- Send in the bailiffs to seize goods to the value of the claim.
- Attachment of earnings so that the award is taken directly from the persons salary
- Charging orders over the defendants property
- Garnishee orders that can order money to be taken from a bank account.

4

PROCEDURE IN THE CROWN COURT

In Chapter 1, we discussed the nature of the Crown Court. As we saw, the Crown Court deals mainly with criminal cases. The process is heavily procedural and each case follows a set pattern. It is not usual for a defendant or prosecution to present a case without the aid of lawyers. Some people, however, choose to do this and the following outlines a case and how it is conducted using a solicitor. The litigant in person will follow exactly the same procedure.

It is highly advisable to have some idea of court procedures before a do-it-yourself presentation of a case. The procedure, however, will remain the same.

The Jury

A jury consists of 12 people and their job is perhaps one of the most important in the whole Crown Court procedure. A Jury is randomly chosen from the local public, between the ages of 18-70 and their job, in a criminal case, is to listen to all the evidence about the facts of a case. They will often have to make hard decisions concerning who to believe or not, when differing versions of what happened are given by the defence and prosecution. At the end of a trial, the jury retires in private and must decide the guilt or innocence of the person charged. The prosecution must prove the case against the defendant on each charge so that the jury are sure of guilt.

The job of a juror can be complicated and disturbing. Quite often, the charges are quite harrowing and the evidence is not that clear. The juror, or jurors, must fight against their own prejudices and must avoid jumping to conclusions.

The following represents basic advice concerning the procedure relating to jurors.

The Court Service produces a booklet called 'You and Your Jury Service'. Further advice can be obtained from the Court Service website. This outlines the role of the juror in more detail. If a court writes to a juror and informs them that they have been selected for jury service, they will send a letter that is filled in stating that either they are able to carry out jury service or asking for reasons why not. The court will:

- Let a juror know at least four weeks before they are needed
- Send a jury summons which sets out the rules about jury service and tells them if they can be let off serving as a juror
- Send a booklet 'You and Your Jury Service' which explains more about the duty of a juror and also details expenses and allowances that can be claimed.

- An information leaflet will be sent which includes a map, details of public transport and where to park, the times of opening, details of refreshments etc.

When a juror arrives at court they will be shown to a separate sitting room for jurors and shown a video which explains the job of a juror in more detail. They can also talk with a customer service officer in private if they wish.

How a jurors time is used

Some people may not be able to sit as jurors on certain trials because, for example, they are connected with the defendant or the case. The court service always summons more jurors than they need because it is difficult to prepare for all circumstances. Normally, a length of service will be five days. Some jurors are needed for all five days others can be let off early. The court service will:

- Try to use time as a juror efficiently
- Tell a juror every hour when you may be needed in court
- Let them go as soon as possible if they are not needed
- Let them go back to work on days or part days when they are not needed, if an employer agrees with this.
- Give the juror a special number to phone (in larger Crown Courts) to find out if they need to come to court that day

Complaining about Jury Service

If a juror wants to complain about jury service then a member of staff will first try to sort out the problems then and there. If they are still not happy they can refer their complaint to the customer service manager. They can also write to the court manager. They may be able to claim compensation if they have run up costs because of court mistakes.

Inside a Crown Court
Court etiquette

All courts are formal. The whole ethos underpinning the dispensation of justice is underpinned by formality. This is because the events that happen within a courtroom are very serious, can lead to the deprivation of liberty and therefore must be treated with an appropriate gravity.

When attending court:

- Remove all headgear before entering the court. There are exceptions for religious observances.
- Enter and leave the courtroom at an appropriate time so as to cause as little disturbance as possible.
- Keep quiet at all times.
- Sit in the designated areas, which will be pointed out to you by the usher.
- Stand when the judge enters or leaves the court.
- Always ask the usher if you are in any doubt as to what to do.

The following activities are not permitted in court:

- Smoking
- Eating and drinking.
- Reading magazines and newspapers.
- Taking photographs.
- Making tape recordings
- Using a mobile phone.
- Using a personal stereo.
- Taking notes (unless authorised to do so by the usher).
- Bringing an animal into court (with the exception of guide dog for the blind).

The Judge

The judge presides over the trial and tries to ensure clarity and fairness. The judge will decide on legal issues such as whether evidence is admissible (i.e. what the jury is allowed to take into account).

The judge must remain apart from other people in a trial and therefore has a separate entrance and a private office called 'Judges chambers'. If you have decided to represent yourself without the aid of a barrister then it is highly likely that the judge will provide some guidance without prejudicing his or her position.

Barristers

We have already discussed the role of barristers and solicitors in chapter one. Barristers (or counsel) are qualified lawyers who represent the prosecution or the defendant (in criminal cases) or the defendant or claimant (in civil cases). Barristers have special training in courtroom procedure and advocacy (presenting cases in court). They sit in the courtroom facing the judge and are responsible for explaining the case, arguing its merits and, most importantly, presenting the case by calling the evidence upon which the case is decided.

Solicitors

Solicitors are qualified lawyers. They work with their client and the barrister, preparing the case and collecting the evidence. Some solicitors have received special training and are qualified to act as advocates in the Crown Court. Solicitors can present cases in the magistrates and county courts. In a criminal case, the defence solicitor is appointed by the defendant. The lawyers representing the prosecution will usually be employed by the Crown Prosecution Service. Solicitors and their employees who assist counsel in the Crown Court sit behind them. In a civil case, each side chooses its own lawyers.

Clerk

The clerk, sometimes called the associate, looks after all the documents for the trial, and records all the judges decisions and instructions, so that they can be acted upon.

The clerk is responsible for some of the most important formalities: he or she reads out the 'indictments' (telling the defendant what he or she is charged with) ensures that the jury takes a solemn oath to give a true verdict according to the evidence and that the witness takes a solemn oath to tell the truth. At the end of the trial they ask the jury what their verdict is. This is called 'taking the verdict'.

The Usher

The usher looks after the courtroom and the people in it including the judge and jury. The usher will also bring into court the defendants, witnesses and others required by the court.

The Crown Prosecution Service

The Crown Prosecution Service work closely with the police and:

- Prosecute people in England and Wales who have been charged by the police with a criminal offence
- Advise the police on possible prosecutions
- Review prosecutions or possible prosecutions
- Review prosecutions started by the police to ensure the right defendants are prosecuted on the right charges before the appropriate court
- Prepare cases for court
- Prosecute cases at magistrate's courts and instruct counsel to prosecute cases in the Crown Court and higher courts.
- Work with others to improve the effectiveness and efficiency of the criminal justice system

The CPS, although working closely with the police is independent of them.

The Defendant

This is the person who has been accused of a crime and is standing trial for this in the court. In a criminal case sometimes two or more people are accused of committing a crime together.

Witnesses

During the trial the witnesses are brought one by one into the witness box to give evidence, i.e. to tell the court what they can about the facts of a case. First, the witnesses for the prosecution are called. Their evidence must be limited to things that they have seen or heard themselves. Experts may also be called on to give authoritative opinions on subjects such as fingerprints, guns or medical matters.

Next, the witnesses for the defence are called. They may include the defendant and other witnesses, including, for example, 'alibi witnesses' (if the defendant denies being present at the scene and the witness can say where he was) and the defences own experts.

If there is no dispute between the prosecution and the defence over the evidence of a witness, the witness is not called and instead the evidence is agreed and read to the jury as 'agreed evidence'.

Where a witness is vulnerable or worried about giving evidence he or she may be supported through the experience by a member of the witness support team. They will look after the witness outside the court and remain in court when the witness is giving evidence.

More details about the witness Support Team can be obtained from the court office.

The press

The press or other representatives of the media usually sit at the front of the public seating area (or in other reserved seats) to report what happens in court for the benefit of the public in general. They are entitled to report any part of the court proceedings providing the reports are accurate and fair.

The court may order that they cannot report on proceedings if there is some good legal reason that they should not do so e.g. if children are involved, or matters of law are being discussed in the absence of the jury.

The Public

Any member of the public may sit in the public seating area to see and hear what is happening.

Court Reporter

Many cases are officially recorded as they proceed by a court reporter who is responsible for recording the evidence and the judges summing-up (in criminal cases) and the judgement (in civil cases).

Dock Officer

In the Crown Court the defendant who is accused of a crime is accompanied by a dock officer who is responsible for his/her security.

The above represent the personnel who are key players in the process of a trial.

We will now look at a case study which will help put the whole trial process in context. is a case study outlining the procedures in a Crown Court trial

Case study

Guide to a criminal case

The following constitutes the procedure in a criminal case.

Background to the case.

Peter, 18, has been arrested and charged with four offences-theft (robbing an off-licence of wine and beer) assault (hitting the shopkeeper in the face and breaking his jaw), possessing an offensive weapon (a knife) and damage to property (breaking a window and damaging shop furniture).

Peter told his lawyers that he didn't do any of the above and he has been set up by the shopkeeper, who knows and dislikes him. He said that he had merely gone into the shop to buy wine and beer, had met a friend and absentmindedly taken beer and wine whilst he was talking, and he was told by the shopkeeper that he would not be served. The shopkeeper attacked him and Peter acted in-self defence. He also stated that he did not have a knife. There was a customer in the shop at the time who saw what happened.

Peter is represented by a solicitor who has 'briefed' or 'instructed' a barrister to act as Peters advocate-that is to present his case in court. Peter will have met the solicitor who is preparing his case on a number of occasions. He will probably meet his barrister for the first time before the trial.

The prosecution are also represented by a barrister briefed by the Crown prosecution Service.

Some weeks ago Peter appeared before the magistrates. Then the prosecution solicitor explained the evidence against him. Peter did not have to say what his explanation was. The magistrates said there was enough evidence for Peter to stand trial in the Crown Court before judge and jury.

The judge runs the trial and must ensure it is conducted fairly at all times. The judge has to decide what evidence can be allowed and what cannot. He or she has to advise the jury what the law is and, if Peter is found guilty, the judge will decide what sentence to give. He or she wears judicial robes (a wig and gown) and remains apart from everyone else involved.

As stated, the jury has to listen to all the evidence about the facts. They will often have to decide which witness to believe or not to believe when different versions of what happened are given by different people. They must then decide, in private, whether the defendant is guilty or not. The prosecution must prove the case against the defendant on each charge so that the jury are sure of guilt.

The procedure

Prosecuting: the charge

Everyone who is accused of a crime must know and understand clearly what it is they are said to have done. This must be in writing.

The clerk reads out each charge and asks Peter if he is guilty or not guilty.

The defence

As the charges are read out, Peter says 'not guilty' to each charge.

The jury is sworn in. Twelve members of the public, selected at random, are asked to swear that they will give a true verdict 'according to the evidence'. The juror has the choice to swear or affirm, depending on religious belief. If Peter has a good reason he can object to any of the jurors. For example, if one is a friend, or a teacher at his old school he can object.

The prosecution opening speech

The barrister appearing for the prosecution will make a short opening speech to the judge and jury telling them what the case is all about. He has to summarise both what the prosecution say happened and what Peter says happened.

Prosecution evidence

Each witness who saw what happened is called to give evidence. Usually the victim goes first. So in this case, the prosecution calls:

- the shopkeeper
- the other customer in the shop
- the police who were called and who arrested Peter
- the doctor who examined the shopkeeper
- the forensic scientist who found Peters fingerprints on the knife.

Each witness swears to tell the truth or affirms that he or she will do so. The prosecution barrister asks questions of these witnesses first. The questions must not suggest the 'right' answer. These are called 'leading questions'. So for example he cannot ask the shopkeeper 'did you see Peter steal the wine and beer' he must ask 'what did you see Peter do?'

Cross- examination

The barrister representing Peter can test the evidence of each of the prosecution's witnesses by asking any questions which are relevant to the case.

It is the best opportunity to show that the witness is unreliable or cannot remember things clearly-or is even dishonest.

When Peters barrister put it to the shopkeeper that he chased Peter and fell down as he reached him, injuring himself, he admitted that he could not be sure whether Peter hit him before he fell or it just felt like that and he was confused. If the defence disagrees with what a witness has said they must make this clear.

The prosecution

When the policeman who arrested Peter said he found the knife in Peters pocket, Peter's barrister has to suggest to him that, as Peter says that he never had a knife, the policeman must have placed it there. Peter's barrister has finished his cross-examination and the defence is asked if they have any further questions. At this point he declines.

The defence opening speech

The defence barrister can make a speech but does not have to and is not allowed to if Peter is the only defence witness on his side. The defence rarely makes a speech at this stage – saving things for later.

The defence evidence

The witnesses on Peter's side now give evidence. Usually the defendant, Peter in this case, goes first.

He does not have to give evidence but if he does not the jury can draw inferences from his failure to do so. The jury may think that he has something to hide, as he was the best-placed person to say what he believed happened.

Cross examination of
defence witnesses

In this case, Peter gives evidence, repeating his story originally given to the police. Other witnesses on Peter's side also give evidence. His only real witness in this case was his friend Dave who he had met in the shop and talked to. Dave confirmed that Peter was notoriously absent minded and would not have deliberately stolen the beer and wine but was indeed only putting them into his bag.

This is the prosecution's opportunity to challenge Peter and any other witness on his side. This can be very direct and personal. The way in which Peter gives his evidence and replies to challenging questions can be the key for the jury to make up their minds on the truth of the case. In this case:

- Peter admitted under questioning that he had an alcohol habit and had treatment for this habit.

- Dave admitted that he knew Peter had bought a knife. He couldn't identify it though as the one the police said that they had found on Peter.

- The other customer maintained that although the shopkeeper was angry and chased after Peter he had not seen Peter hit him.

Prosecution closing speech

The prosecution barrister takes a final speech to the jury explaining how he says the charges are proved.

Defence closing speech

The defence barrister makes a closing speech and explains to the jury why he says that the evidence does not amount to sure proof that Peter did what he is accused of.

Judges summing up

The judge first tells the jury what the law is on each charge and what the prosecution must prove in order to make the jury sure of the case. He then reminds them of the important parts of the evidence from both sides. This must be fair and balanced.

Reaching a verdict

The jury will retire to a separate room. This will be guarded by a 'jury bailiff' who is an usher. The jury must elect a 'foreman' of the jury who will act as an unofficial chair and will announce the verdict in court. Juries must not discuss the case with anyone else, even if they go home overnight.

Juries are expected to reach a unanimous verdict. If they have tried for a long time the judge can agree to accept a majority verdict which must be at least 10-2. If that is not possible the jury is said to disagree and the defendant must go through a retrial. If the same thing happens a second time the custom is that the prosecution is dropped and the defendant is found not guilty.

The verdict

If the jury finds the defendant not guilty then he can leave the court immediately as a free man. He cannot then be tried again for the same offence (although there are currently proposals to change this in certain circumstances).

If he is found guilty the judge must pass sentence. In this case, Peter is found guilty of theft and possessing an offensive weapon, but he is found not guilty of assault.

The judge now has to sentence Peter. He will take everything he knows about the case into account. He will be told if Peter has any previous convictions. He will not sentence Peter until he has received pre-sentence reports from the probation service.

Plea in mitigation

Peter's barrister can explain to the judge why a light sentence is more appropriate than a severe one. He can produce references for him and explain any relevant personal circumstances about work or family life. The judge will also have a pre-sentence report prepared by a probation officer. All of this can be very important in helping a judge to decide between a sentence of custody and some other punishment.

Sentence

In this case Peter has past convictions for stealing and violence. He has been fined and placed on probation. The judge has the following choices:

- Rehabilitation (probation)

- Community punishment (unpaid work on behalf of the community

- Custody in a young offender institution (Peter is under 21 so cannot be sent to prison)

- As Peter's offences include theft, violence and possessing an offensive weapon, and he has a previous conviction he is sentenced to eight months in a young offender institution.

The dock officer who has been escorting peter to the dock will take him down to the courts cells prior to transferring him to an institution.

Refer overleaf to summary of trial process.

Summary of trial process in the Crown Court

1. Prosecution – the charge is read to the defendant.
2. The defendant pleads guilty or not guilty.
3. The prosecution makes the opening speech.
4. The prosecution gives evidence. Witnesses are called.
5. The defendant's barrister cross-examines the prosecution witnesses.
6. The defence barrister makes an opening speech.
7. The defence calls witnesses.
8. The prosecution cross-examines witnesses for the defence.
9. The prosecution makes a closing speech to the jury.
10. The defence makes a closing speech to the jury.
11. The judge sums up the case.
12. The jury retire to reach a verdict.
13. The verdict is announced.
14. The defence barrister can make a plea in mitigation.
15. The judge will pass sentence.

5

PROCEDURE IN THE COUNTY COURTS

In chapter one, we briefly discussed the nature of county courts. In this chapter, we will look at county courts in more depth and also the procedure in a civil case, much as we looked at the procedure in a criminal case in the previous chapter. The case study outlined will help to outline the civil case procedure, specifically in relation to personal compensation. In the following chapter, we will look in depth at making a small claim for faulty goods and services.

County Courts

These courts were created by the County Courts Act 1846. They deal with the majority of the civil disputes, acting as local courts dealing with small claims. There are 54 "circuits" or areas in the country, each circuit having one or more judges assigned to it, resulting in about 400 courts in England and Wales

The civil procedure rules

County courts are governed by the Civil Procedure Rules which guide the actions of the county courts and of claimants and defendants.

Circuit judges

Circuit judges were created by the Courts Act 1971 and are appointed from barristers of at least 10 years standing.

Registrars

Registrars conduct the administrative work of county courts. They are civil servants and must be solicitors of seven years standing. They have jurisdiction to try cases where the amount is less than £500 pounds

County Court jurisdiction

County courts have a range of responsibilities:

- Hearing cases and tort (negligence) up to £5000 pounds, although there is no limit if both parties agree
- Housing and landlord and tenant disputes-the court will consider cases where the title to land and recovery of possession of land, concerns a net annual value for rating of less than £2000 pounds. The court also decides on matters under the Rent Act 1977, the Landlord and Tenant Act 1954 (Business tenancies), the Housing Acts 1985, 1988 and 1996
- The County Court will also hear matters where an aggrieved person has a statutory right or legal right of appeal in housing matters
- Considering matters of equity such as trusts, mortgages and dissolution of partnerships where the amount is less than £30,000 pounds

- Hearing petitions for bankruptcy and winding up of companies with a paid up share capital not exceeding £20,000 pounds
- Uncontested hearings under the Matrimonial Causes Act 1967, or Nullity of marriage. If they are contested they will be transferred to the High Court
- Hearing disputes concerning the grant of probate or letters of administration, where the estate of the deceased person is less than £15,000 pounds

The jurisdiction of the County Court is limited to the locality it is in: cases should be commenced in the court in the area where the defendant resides or carries on business or where the cause of the action arises. There are more than three times as many proceedings commenced in the County Court than in all the divisions of the High Court which deals with all other Civil Disputes

Small Claims procedure
The County court hears small claims actions up to £50,000 pounds although over £3,000 it is likely to be heard by a Tribunal. We will be discussing small claims in more depth later on in this book.

Tribunals
The enormous growth in the work of the courts in modern times, coupled with the relatively high costs of bringing a court action, has led to an increase of the number of tribunals. Tribunals deal with disputes in particular areas of the law and

attempt to do so in a less formal and speedier manner than would be possible through the ordinary courts

Tribunals are independent and impartial bodies, using the same rules of evidence under oath as the ordinary courts, although the Tribunal members may comprise both legally qualified and lay members. Procedures may be heard in a Tribunal having been referred from a court

Civil cases in the County Court

We have seen, in the previous chapter that trials in the Crown, or High, Courts are usually trials by jury and the Crown Prosecution Service is involved.

Cases in the county courts are cases held without jury, with the judge having the final say. This is because the county courts deal with non-criminal matters, small claims, between individuals and organisations. As with the High Court, the procedure is formal and regulated and there is a set process to go through when preparing and presenting a claim. In the county court, the person taking the case to court is called the 'claimant' and the person defending is called the 'defendant'. Neither party has to be represented by a solicitor. Many people who use the county courts chose to present their own cases. As we have seen, although this can be the case in the High court it is not the norm.

In the next chapter there is an outline of the small claims procedure relating to money judgements. In these cases, a solicitor is not usually used. However, in many other cases, a solicitor is used and the following case outlines the procedure where a person is defended.

Case study outlining the county court procedure

Sandra was in the women's toilet at an airport. The airport is controlled by the British Airports Authority. She entered a cubicle and locked the door after her. However, when she tried to get out she found that the door would not open. Sandra panicked, as she realised that her flight was leaving very soon. She decided to clamber over the top of the door, as her cries for help went unheeded. She stood on the door handle, which snapped and she fell backwards, badly spraining her wrist and breaking her ankle.

Sandra decided to claim compensation from the BAA stating that they were negligent and to blame for the faulty lock. In short, they are responsible for her injury and subsequent missed flight and time off work.

On reflection, Sandra has decided to instruct a firm of solicitors to act for her. She knows that she can represent herself in the county court but has decided that the matter might get complicated and that the BAA will pay more attention to a firm of solicitors.

Before the case goes to court, Sandra's solicitors must fill in a claim form and send this to court. The claim form is the form used to start all cases in the county court and sets out Sandra's version of events and states why she is entitled to compensation.

The British Airports Authority disputes the claim and have to present their defence. This sets out their case and states why Sandra should not receive any compensation.

Both sides may obtain evidence – that is statements from witnesses to support their side of the case, which sets out what they say happened.

As Sandra is claiming less than £15,000 compensation and the case should be dealt with quickly, it is heard in the local county court before a district judge. If it involved more than £15,000 or was seen to be more complicated it would be heard either in a county court by a more senior judge or in the High Court by a High Court Judge, but the proceedings would be similar.

As explained, there is no jury in most civil cases – so the judge hears the case on his or her own. The judge will have been involved in the early stages of the case making sure that both sides have their cases ready for trial. Judges now have to 'manage' cases they are going to hear in order to make sure they are dealt with as quickly and efficiently as possible. In court the judge must decide on the basis of the evidence what has actually happened and then has to apply the law to settle who was actually responsible. If the case is proved the judge will decide how much compensation to award to Sandra.

In a civil trial a claimant does not have to make the judge sure that he or she is right. They have to prove the case on a 'balance of probabilities'. This means that their case is more often right than not. The judge will wear judicial robes and a wig and will sit apart from everyone else.

The case

> ### Claimant's opening speech

At the outset of the case, Sandra's solicitor makes a short opening speech to the court which explains what the case is and what evidence will be called to prove it. The solicitor will also summarise what the defendant says the position is.

> ### Claimant's evidence

The claimant – Sandra – is usually called to give evidence first and says what happened. Other witnesses who help her to prove her claim give evidence. So here, her lawyer calls:

- her friend who had been waiting for her outside. She had eventually gone back into the toilet and heard Sandra in pain in the locked cubicle
- the doctor who examined her and reported on her injuries
- other people who had used the toilet in the recent past and had reported that the lock was sometimes jamming and defective.

An important piece of evidence here, perhaps the most important piece, was the state of the lock-was it faulty or was it a one-off incident, not down to negligence.

This is something an expert can decide and the court has ordered a single expert to examine the state of the lock and report on the problem. This saves arguments between different experts on what should be an uncomplicated technical matter. The expert said that, in this case, the lock was faulty.

Cross examination

This is where the lawyer representing the defendant (the counsel) will test what has been said by the claimant and witnesses. It is an opportunity to show that their memory is shaky or the evidence was exaggerated or made up. The questions can be very direct or personal.

In this case, Sandra accepts that she must have realised that the door handle was probably not going to withstand her weight and could break. Therefore, she knowingly put herself at risk.

Re-examination

This is a chance for Sandra's solicitor to ask further questions to clear up any confusion. However, he cannot ask about new things.

Defendants opening speech

The barrister representing the Airports Authority can make a short speech introducing the evidence he is going to call. However, often the witnesses are called straight away.

Defendant's evidence

The witnesses on the Airport Authority's side now give evidence. In this case, an employee of the BAA gives evidence as to how often the toilets are checked for damage to doors. In addition, he gives evidence concerning any other reports of people being trapped.

The employee explains that if Sandra had called out it would have been heard quite clearly by a number of people and explained that he had heard nothing until Sandra's friend had reported the problem.

The Airport Authority accepted the expert's evidence that at the time he inspected the lock it was faulty and the doctor's evidence about Sandra's injuries.

Cross examination

This is the opportunity for Sandra's solicitors to challenge the defendant's witnesses. The employee of BAA admitted that, as he was concentrating on other things at the time he probably would not have heard the cries for help, unless it was very loud.

In addition, the records did not show that the lock had been inspected or who had carried out the checks. So Sandra's solicitor suggested that there was real doubt about whether there had been an effective recent inspection.

Defendant's closing speech

The Airport Authority's barrister now makes a speech to the court which reviews all the evidence and explains why the BAA says that it wasn't reasonable for them to be held responsible for Sandra's injuries.

He says that the BAA accepts that the lock was faulty but they had carried out all reasonable checks and, at the end of the day, although Sandra was injured, in some respects this was down to her own actions not the BAA's negligence. The barrister will explain to the jury the relevant law and how it should be applied in this case.

Claimant's closing speech

Sandra's solicitor now makes the final speech. He explains that the BAA admitted that they were responsible for the lock and that the evidence show that 'in all likelihood' they had not checked it properly to see that it was safe. Unlike a criminal case in the Crown Court, Sandra does not have to prove this so that the judge is sure-it is enough to prove that, on a balance of probabilities the locks were not checked.

He also argues that Sandra should not be blamed for trying to escape when the problem was caused by the negligence of the BAA in the first place.

He describes to the judge what the law is and refers to any relevant cases which have been decided in similar situations, whether they support his case or not. The relevant similar findings are called 'precedents'.

Judgement

The judge now gives his judgement. Usually this happens straightaway but in more complicated cases the judgement can be reserved and given at a later date when the judge has had a chance to consider everything in detail.

In this case, the judge said that this was a simple case. He decided that the BAA were responsible for providing safe changing rooms in the sports centre. He had considered the evidence about checking the locks and that in his view it was more probable than not that this lock hadn't been checked recently. Finally, the judge said that it was reasonable for someone trapped in a cubicle to try to escape provided their efforts were sensible.

The decision was that the BAA should compensate Sandra. However, he also decided that Sandra had been at fault. She had contributed to her own injuries by her own negligence in risking standing on a 'moveable' object-the door handle. The judge ruled that Sandra's own compensation of £4750 should be reduced by 20% because she had also been at fault. She was therefore awarded £3800.

The above is an outline of a typical county court case. It can be seen, however, that the procedures in the High Courts and country courts have one thing in common. They are bound by formality and involve a set procedure where each party can present their case, either through representatives or on their own behalf, and each can expect to get a full hearing. In the Crown Courts, a jury will, in most cases, make a decision as to innocence and guilt. In the county courts, the judge will do so. However, the processes are similar in many respects.

Refer overleaf for a summary of the trial process in the county court.

Summary of trial process in the county court.

1. The claimant or the claimant's solicitor makes an opening speech.
2. The claimant is called to give evidence.
3. The defendant or the defendant's solicitor cross-examines the claimant.
4. There is a re-examination.
5. The defendant or defendant's solicitor makes an opening speech.
6. The defendant gives evidence.
7. There is a cross examination of the defendant.
8. The defendant or defendant's solicitor makes a closing speech.
9. The claimant or claimant's solicitor makes a closing speech.
10. The judge gives his judgement.

6

USING THE COUNTY COURT COMMENCING A SMALL CLAIM

Having looked briefly at the operations of the legal system, it is now necessary to examine the processes involved in commencing a small claim in the county court. Although a claim depends on the subject matter, the majority of people tend to take action in the county court small claims division.

Commencing a claim

A person can start legal action in any court and if the case is defended the court will decide what procedure to use. If the case is a simple one, with a value of £5000 or less, the court will decide that the small claims procedure will be used and will allocate the case to the small claims track. In most cases, the court will not order that costs are paid by the losing party in a small claims case. For this reason, most people do not use a solicitor when making a small claim. It may, however, be possible to get legal help using the legal help scheme.

Types of case dealt with in the small claims track

When the court is considering whether to allocate the case to a small claims track it will take into account a number of factors, but the main factor is the value of the case. If the value of a case

71

is £5000 or less it will generally be allocated to the small claims track. However, if it is a personal injury claim, it will be allocated to the small claims track only if the value of the claim for the personal injuries is not more than £1000. If the claimant is a tenant and is claiming against their landlord because repairs are needed to the premises and the cost of the work is £1000 or less, the case will be allocated to the small claims track.

Types of claims in the small claims court

The most common types of small claims are:

- Compensation for faulty goods, for example washing machines or other goods that go wrong
- Compensation for faulty services provided, for example by builders, garages and so on
- Disputes between landlords and tenants, for examples, rent arrears, compensation for not doing repairs
- Wages owed or money in lieu of notice

If a case proves to be too complex then a judge may refer the case to another track for a full hearing, even if below the limit for that track.

Actions before applying to court

As we saw in the previous chapter, before applying to court it is always necessary to try to solve the problem amicably, or as amicably as possible without recourse to legal action. A person who intends to commence a claim should write a 'letter before action' which should set out terms for settlement before applying to court.

For example, if a television is defective, or workmanship on a car is faulty, there is no point applying to court for compensation before contacting the garage or repair shop. Whilst this may seem obvious, there are cases where people do rush in. Always try to settle before launching court action. It will assist in the case if it does go to court.

Which court deals with a small claim

The court action can be started in any court, but the case can be transferred. If the claim is defended and the claim is for a fixed amount, the court will automatically transfer the case to a defendant's local court (if he or she is an individual not a company). In other cases, either party can ask for the case to be transferred.

Commencing a claim

The claimant commences a claim by filling in a claim form, obtainable from local county courts or legal stationers. They can also be obtained from the internet. The government court site is www.Courtservice.gov.uk. All forms can be obtained from this website as can a host of information on all legal topics.

The form is quite straightforward and asks for details of claimant and defendant and how much is owed. The form also asks for the particulars of the claim. The particulars set out full details of the claim. If there is not enough room on the form then a separate piece of paper can be used. The claimant has a right to spend a little more time on the particulars and can send them to the defendant separately, but no later than 14 days after the claim form.

The forms are designed to be user friendly and are accompanied by guidance notes to ensure that no mistakes are made.

The claimant may be entitled to claim interest on the claim and, if so, must give details of the interest claimed in the particulars of claim. In a personal injury claim the particulars of claim must include the claimants date of birth and brief details of the injuries. The claimant must attach a list of any past expenses and losses that they want to claim for and any expenses and losses that they may incur in the future.

Applying for the claim form to be issued

The claimant must ensure that two copies of the claim form reach the court where court action is to commence and a copy should be kept for records. There will be a fee to pay. Currently this depends on the amount of money to be claimed. You should check with your local county court, small claims division, for the current fees.

In some cases, the fee will be waived, for example if the claimant is receiving income support, working families tax credit, disabled persons tax credit or income based job seekers allowance. If none of these benefits are received, but financial hardship would be suffered if a fee was paid, the fee may also be waived. The court will stamp the claim form and then, in most cases, serve it on the defendant. The court will give the claimant a notice of issue.

Usually the court will serve the claim form by sending it to the defendant by first class post. The claimant will be deemed to have received it on the second day of posting. If the claimant wishes to serve the claim form his or herself then a request should be made and the court will provide the form and other forms that go with it.

If the case is not defended

If the defendant is not defending the case, then he or she may accept that they owe the money. If this is the case then he or she can pay the money directly to the claimant. If the defendant has accepted that they owe the money, but needs time to pay, they can propose an arrangement, for example that the amount owed is paid in instalments or all the money in one lump sum on a specified future date. If the claimant accepts this offer, he or she will have to return a form to the court requesting 'judgement by admission'. If the defendant does not keep to this agreement the claimant can then take enforcement action.

If the claimant does not accept this offer then he or she must give good reason and a court official will decide what a reasonable arrangement will be. The court will send both parties an order for payment. If the claimant is not happy with the order then he or she will have to write to the court giving reasons and sending a copy to the defendant. A judge will then decide what is reasonable for the defendant to pay. If the defendant does not keep to the arrangement, the claimant can take enforcement action.

If the defendant is defending the case

If the case is to be defended, the defendant has to respond to the claim within 14 days of service (this is the second day of posting). If the particulars of claim were served after the claim form the defendant must respond within 14 days of service of particulars of claim. A defence is launched by the defendant sending back the defence form, which was sent with the claim form.

If the defendant does not send a defence back within the time period then the claimant can ask for an order to be made against him or her.

The defendant can send the defence back to the court or can send the acknowledgement of service form sent with the defence form back to court and the defence form back within 14 days of this. This helps if more time is needed.

When the defence is sent to the court the court will send an allocation questionnaire to both the claimant and the defendant. This must be returned to the court no later than the date specified in it. When the claimant returns the allocation form a fee should also be sent although this can be waived on financial grounds. The court will use the information contained within the allocation questionnaire to decide which track to allocate the case to.

When the court has decided to allocate the case to the small claims track, the claimant and defendant will be sent a notice of allocation. This form will tell the parties what they have to do to prepare for the hearing. These instructions are called 'directions'. One example of directions may be that parties are told that they should send all copies of relevant documents to court, documents that they intend to use in court in the case against the other party. These are sent at least 14 days before the case begins. There are standard directions for a number of common cases, for example, if the claim is to do with a holiday then there will be standard directions from the courts as to the evidence needed.

The day of the hearing

The notice of allocation will usually specify the time, day and date of hearing, where the hearing will take place and how much time has been allowed for it. If the claimant wants to attend the hearing but for some reason cannot, then a letter should be sent to the court requesting a different hearing date. A fee is payable and the court will only agree to this request if it is based on reasonable grounds.

A claimant can also ask the court to deal with a claim in his or her absence, A typical case might be where the costs and time to reach the court are disproportionate. If this is the case then a letter should reach the court at least seven days before the case. In some cases, the court will not set a final hearing date. The following are alternatives used by the courts:

- The court could propose that the case is dealt with without a hearing. If both parties have no objections then the case can be decided on the papers only. If the parties do not reply by the date given then the court will usually take that silence as consent

- The court may hold a preliminary hearing. This could happen if the claim requires special directions which the judge wants to explain to the parties personally or where the judge feels that the claimant or defendant has no real prospect of succeeding and wants to sort out the claim as soon as possible to save everyone time and expense, or if the papers do not show any reasonable grounds for bringing the claim. A preliminary hearing could become a final hearing where the case is decided.

Preparing a case

It is important that a case is prepared carefully – the court has to be convinced. A reasonable amount of time should be spent ensuring that all the facts are entered, all dates specified and all paperwork is available. The following points are a general guide to what preparation should be made:

- someone with low income can use the legal help scheme to cover the costs of legal advice, but not representation from a solicitor. This advice can be extremely useful and can include getting expert reports, for example on faulty goods. However, a report can only be used in court with permission of the court

- notes about the case should be set out in date order. This will help you to present your case and will make sense to a judge. All backing documentation should

- be taken to court and be presented if asked for. This documentation should be organised around the presentation, in chronological order

- damaged or faulty goods should be taken as evidence. If it is not possible to do this then photographs should be taken instead

- evidence of expenses should be taken along and any receipts kept

- all letters about the case should be taken to court

- in most cases, the claimant and defendant may be the only witnesses. If the court has agreed that other witnesses can attend, then they must attend. If a witness has difficulty getting time off work then a witness summons can be served. The courts will explain how to do this.

The final hearing

The final hearing is usually held in public but can be held in private if the parties agree or the judge thinks that it is necessary. Hearings in the small claims track are informal and the usual rules of evidence do not apply. The judge can adopt any method of dealing with the hearing that he or she thinks fit and can also ask questions of the witnesses before anyone else. A lay representative has the right to speak on behalf of a person at a hearing but only if that party attends the hearing. If an interpreter is needed, because English is not the first language then an experienced advisor should be consulted, or the court may be able to advise on this.

At the end of the hearing the judge will pass judgement. The judge has to give reasons for the decision that he or she has arrived at. If the claimant wins, he or she will get the court fee back as well as the sum awarded. If the claimant loses no fees will be returned. However, it is unlikely that any other costs will have to be paid.

Appealing against a decision

A party may appeal against a judgement in the small claims track only if the court made a mistake in law or there was a serious irregularity in the proceedings. If a person wishes to appeal then a notice of appeal must be filed within 14 days. A fee is payable although this can be waived in cases of financial hardship. If you do wish to appeal a decision, it is very likely that you would need to consult a solicitor or an experienced advisor to help you.

Enforcement of orders

If a defendant does not pay, the claimant can go back to court and enforce that order. As we have seen, there are a number of remedies, such as bailiff, attachment of earnings and garnishee order. Another fee is involved when enforcing. The court will give you full details of different remedies and fees involved.

Useful addresses

The Court Services Secretariat
The Lord Chancellors Department
Southside
105 Victoria Street
London SW1E 6QT
Tel: 020 7210 2059

Crown Prosecution Service
50 Ludgate Hill
London EC4M 7EX
Tel: 020 7831 8152

The Free Representation Unit
49-51 Bedford Row
London WC1R 4LR
Tel: 020 7831 0692

The Institute of Legal Executives
Kempston Manor
Kempston
Bedford MK42 7AB
Tel: 01234 8413000

The Law Society
113 Chancery lane
London WC2A 1PL
Tel: 020 7242 1222

Legal Action Group
242 Pentonville Road
London N1 9UN
Tel: 020 7833 8931
National Association of Citizen Advice Bureaus
115-123 Pentonville Road
London N1 9LZ
Tel: 020 7833 8931

The Legal Services Commission
85 Gray's Inn Road
London WC1X 8TX
Tel: 020 7759 0000

Solicitors Complaints Bureau
Portland House
Stag Place
London SW1E 5BL

Glossary of terms

Acknowledgement of service
Form of reply to, or acknowledgement of, a service of court papers.

Acquittal
Discharge of defendant following verdict or direction of not guilty.

Adjourned generally
Temporary suspension of the hearing of a case by a court for a short period.

Advocate
A barrister or solicitor representing a person in court.

Affidavit
A written statement of evidence on oath or by affirmation to be true.

Appeal
Application to a higher court or authority for a review of a lower court decision.

Appellant
Person who appeals

Attachment of earnings

An order that directs an employer of a debtor to deduct a regular amount from salary or wages to pay off a debt.

Bail

Release of a defendant from custody until his or her appearance in court, usually on the basis of financial security.

Bar

The collective term for barristers

Barrister

A member of the bar, that part of the legal profession that has rights of audience before a judge.

Bench warrant

A warrant issued by a judge for the arrest of an absent defendant.

Bill of indictment

A written statement of the charges against a defendant on trial in the Crown Court and signed by an officer of the court.

Brief

Written instructions to counsel to appear at a hearing of a party prepared by the solicitor and setting out the case and any case law relied upon.

Chambers

Either a private room or court where the public are not allowed and where the judge hears a case or offices used by a barrister.

Circuit judge

A judge who sits in the County and/or High Court.

Civil matters

Matters concerning private rights and not offences of the state.

Claim

Proceedings issued in the County or High Courts which initiate an action.

Claimant

The person issuing the claim, previously known as the plaintiff.

Committal

Committal for trial or sentence or an order to be committed to prison.

Common law

The law established over time by precedent.

Conditional discharge

A discharge of a convicted defendant without sentence on condition that he or she does not re-offend within a period of time.

Co-respondent
A person named as an adulterer (or third person) in a divorce.

Counsel
A Barrister

Counterclaim
A claim made by a defendant against a claimant in a case.

County Court
County courts deal with civil matters including all small claims up to £15,000.

Court of Appeal
Divided into civil and criminal divisions and hears appeals from the High court and the County court.

Crown Court
The Crown Court deals with all crimes committed for judgement to the magistrates court and also hears appeals in cases heard by the magistrates court.

Damages
An amount of money claimed as compensation for physical or material loss e.g. personal injury

Defendant
The person standing trial, the person being sued.

Deposition
A statement of evidence written down and sworn or affirmed.

Determination
The scrutiny of a bill of costs in criminal proceedings in order to determine that the amounts claimed are reasonable.

Discovery of documents
The mutual disclosure of evidence and information held by each side relating to a case.

District judge
A judicial officer of the court.

Exhibit
Item or document referred to in an affidavit or used during the court trial or hearing.

Expert witness
Person employed to give evidence on a subject or matter on which they are knowledgeable and qualified.

Fiat
A decree or command

Garnishee
A summons issued by a claimant against a third party for seizure of money or assets in their keeping.

High Court
A civil court which consists of three divisions, the Queens Bench Division, hearing civil disputes, Family Division concerning matrimonial and child related matters and the Chancery dealing with property and fraud related matters.

Indictable offence
A criminal offence triable only by the Crown Court.

Injunction
An order of the court either restraining a person from carrying out a course of action or directing a course of action to be complied with.

Judge
An officer appointed to administer the law and who has the authority to hear and try cases in a court of law.

Jury
A body of jurors sworn to reach a verdict according to evidence presented in court.

Justice of the peace
A lay-magistrate or person appointed to administer business in a magistrates court. Also sits in the crown court with a judge or a recorder to hear appeals and commute sentences.

Law lords
Describes the judges of the House of Lords.

Legal aid/help
Facility to obtain aid towards fees and expenses relating to court cases.

Libel
A written and published statement/article which contains damaging remarks about another persons character and reputation.

Litigation
Legal proceedings.

Lord Chancellor
The cabinet minister who acts as speaker of the House of Lords and oversees the hearings of the Law Lords. Has other wide responsibilities.

Lord Chief Justice
Senior judge of the Court of Appeal Criminal Division and also heads the Queens Bench Division of the High Courts of Justice.

Magistrates Court
A court where criminal proceedings are commenced. Also has jurisdiction to deal with a range of civil matters.

Master of the Rolls
Senior judge of the Court of Appeal Criminal Division.

Mitigation

Reasons submitted on behalf of a guilty party in order to excuse or partly excuse the offence committed in order to minimise the sentence.

Motion

An application by one party to the High Court for a judgement in their favour.

Notary public

Someone who is authorised to swear oaths and execute deeds.

Oath

A verbal promise by a person of religious beliefs to tell the truth.

Official solicitor

A solicitor or barrister appointed by the Lord Chancellor working in the Lord Chancellors office. The duties include looking after the affairs of people who cannot look after affairs due to incapacity i.e. mental illness.

Oral examination

A method of questioning a person under oath before an officer of the court to obtain details of their financial affairs.

Order

A direction of the court.

Particulars of claim
Details relevant to a case

Party
Any of the participants in a court case.

Penal notice
Directions attached to a court order if breach of that order result in imprisonment.

Personal application
Application made to the court without legal representation.

Plea
A defendants reply to a charge.

Pleadings
Documents setting out the claim or defence of parties involved in legal proceedings.

Precedent
The decision of a case which has established principles and which can be used as authority for a future case.

Pre-trial review
A preliminary appointment at which the district judge examines the issues and issues directions and a timetable for the case.

Queens Counsel

Barristers of at least ten years standing, they take on work of importance and are know as 'Silks'.

Recorder

Members of the legal profession (barristers or solicitors) who are appointed to act in a senior capacity on a part time basis and who may progress to the post of full time judge.

Registrar

Known now as district judge and deputy district judges they are active in the county courts.

Right of audience

Entitlement to appear in front of a court in a legal capacity and conduct proceedings.

Solicitor

Member of the legal profession chiefly concerned with representing clients and preparing cases.

Summary judgement

Judgement obtained from the claimant where there is no defence or no valid grounds for defence.

Summing up

A review of the evidence by representatives of the claimant and defendant before the jury retires to give its verdict.

Tort

A civil wrong committed against a person for which compensation may be sought.

Verdict

The finding of guilty or not guilty by a jury.

Witness

A person who gives evidence to court.

APPENDIX 1

COURT CHARTERS

1

COURTS CHARTER FOR THE CIVIL COURTS

This leaflet sets out the standard of service we aim to give you and how you can let us know if you're not happy. We set the standards after talking to people who have used the court. Most people coming to court will be worried about what to expect. We aim to reduce these worries by giving a good, friendly service. When you come to court you can expect fair and equal treatment, no matter what your race, ethnic origin, disability, sex, sexuality or religious beliefs.

If you're coming to court

When we ask you to come to court we'll send you, or your lawyer:

- a map of how to get to court;
- a leaflet with details of public transport and any car parks near the court;
- the times the court is open;
- information on refreshments, telephones, separate waiting areas and so on;
- the name and phone number of our Customer Service Officer.

Before the date of your hearing you can ask to see the type of room or court where your case will be heard. If you can't hear very well and you need help at your court hearing, please speak to our Customer Service Officer who will tell you how we can help you. We can't provide foreign language interpreters, but our staff will tell you who you should contact if you need an interpreter.

The court building is open from 9am on days when we've arranged hearings. The public counter or enquiry point is open from l0am to 4pm. When you come to court you'll find:

- polite, helpful staff wearing name badges;
- clear signs to help you find your way round;
- information leaflets on display;
- a notice giving the name of our Customer Service Officer who will be pleased to help you with any special needs, suggestions or complaints.

When you go to the public counter or enquiry point we will:

- respect your privacy;
- talk to you out of the hearing of other members of the public, if you prefer deal with your question within 10 minutes;
- explain the delay if you have to wait longer.

You can call us between 9am and 5pm and we will :

- answer the phone quickly and helpfully;
- say who you're speaking to;
- will give you a clear and helpful answer.

When you write to the court, and we need to reply, we will:

- write to you or phone you within 10 working days;
- tell you who's writing and tell you how to phone them.

- You will normally have to pay a court fee to begin a case. Please tell us if you can't afford this and you may be able to pay a reduced fee or not pay at all.

If you want to start a case we will:

- send out the documents relating to your case within 10 working days from when you ask us to start;
- tell you the reference number of your case within 10 working days;
- tell you the date you must come to court (if we can).

Money Claim Online

You can start some cases via a secure Internet connection. Fixed money claims up to £100,000 (but not where the sum claimed is yet to be decided) can be started using the Court Service's Money Claim Online at www. court service. Court fees are payable online using a credit or debit card and lots of help and guidance on both the online service and the small claims procedure more generally is available at We can give you forms and help you fill them in but we can't give you legal advice or tell you what to say .We won't be able to say if your case is likely to succeed, or tell you what the judge will decide. When you arrive at Court we'll:

- show on a notice board where your case will be heard;
- arrange for you to wait apart from the other side's witnesses if there isn't a separate area;

- deal with your case as Soon as possible. But delays can happen, for example if the case before yours takes longer than planned.

If you have to wait we'll:

- tell you regularly how much longer you may have to wait;
- tell you as Soon as possible if your case can't be heard that day.

Your hearing

If we have to change the date of your hearing we'll let you know as soon as possible. If your case is defended, a judge will decide how long you should be allowed to prepare for the final hearing or trial and when it will take place. This is called judicial case management. Some cases are more complicated and need more preparation than others. To allow for this, the judge can allocate your case to one of 3 tracks. These are:

- the small claims track;
- the fast track;
- the multi-track.

Allocating your case to a track

Cases allocated to the small claims track are likely to involve fairly small amounts of money and need less preparation. Cases allocated to the multi-track usually involve large amounts of money and a number of witnesses and experts.

To help the judge decide which is the right track for your case you'll be asked to fill in a questionnaire. So will the person you're claiming against. It will ask things like how much you're claiming, if you want to use witnesses or an expert and so on. When the judge sees the questionnaire, they will make a decision. This will be in a notice of allocation and it will tell you what you have to do to get your case ready for the final hearing and the time you should do this by.

If your case is allocated to the small claims track, the notice wilt usually tell you the time, date and place where the hearing will take place. If your case is allocated to the fast track, the notice will usually tell you in which period of time you can expect your trial to start.

Court decisions and orders

You may ask us to enter a judgment because a defendant hasn't replied to the claim. If we can do this, we'll make the judgment and, if necessary, tell you and the defendant within I 0 working days from then. If you've used Money Claim Online, you can also ask us to enter judgment online.

The judge may hear your case in court or make a decision based on the documents relating to your case. We will send you an order setting out the judge's decision within I0 working days from the date the decision was made.

You can ask us to cancel the registration of a judgment against you. If you pay what you owe within one month from the date of the judgment, we'll send out a certificate of cancellation. We will do this within 5 working days from when we get your request and proof you've paid.

If you pay what you owe more than one month after the judgment, you can ask us to mark the judgment as satisfied. If you can't give us proof you've paid, we'll contact the claimant (the person who brought the case against you) to find out if you've paid.

If you choose to try another way, we'll prepare and send the documents within 10 working days from when you pay us the fee. For major companies who use our computer system at the County Court Bulk Centre, or who issue online through Money Claim Online, we'll:

- send claim forms to defendants within 48 hours from when we get the information
- send judgments to defendants within 48 hours from when they are made;
- send warrants of execution to the appropriate court within 48 hours.
-

Community Legal Services

The CLS will help you decide the type of legal advice you need. Telephone 020 7759 0000 email address on their website. website www.justask.org.uk

Getting debts paid

Before you decide to enforce a court order (try to get the judgment paid), you should remember that we can't guarantee you'll get your money back. We can give you information on the different ways you can try to get your money back and the fees you'll have to pay. If you ask us to send a warrant of execution to a bailiff (which allows them to remove and sell goods to try to pay your claim or obtain an offer of payment) we'll:

- send it out within I 0 working days from when you pay us the fee;
- make sure the bailiff visits the defendant within I5 working days from when we send out the warrant if the defendant doesn't pay;
- send you a report within one month after we send out the warrant;
- report to you every month after that until the bailiff has made a final report;
- send you the report within 5 working days from when we get it.

If you issued your claim and obtained your judgment online using Money Claim Online, you can apply for a warrant of execution online. If you ask us to, we'll tell you how much money a particular court has collected under warrants of execution. Please ask our staff for information about the other ways you can try to get your money back there and then. If you're still not happy, you can speak to our Customer Service Manager or Court Manager. If you prefer, you can write to the

Court Manager of the court in question. All complaints will be dealt with quickly and efficiently. We welcome suggestions and compliments too. If you'd like a complaint form, please ask one of our staff. For more information visit our website at www.courtservice.gov.uk

We can investigate complaints about how a judge behaved in court but we can't investigate anything to do with their judgment, their assessment of the evidence or any of the decisions they made about the handling of your case. These can only be challenged by way of appeal.

Neither the Department for Constitutional Affairs nor anyone else has the power to investigate or overturn the decisions of the courts and there are no circumstances in which we can consider complaints about judges' decisions

Complaints about the personal conduct of judges should be sent in writing to:

Judicial Correspondence Unit
Department for Constitutional Affairs
PO Box 38528
5th Floor
30 Millbank
London SWIP4XB
Telephone: 020 7217 4840
Fax: 020 7217 4875

Citizens Advice Bureaux

Give free, confidential impartial and independent advice on a limitless range of subjects, including debt, benefits, housing, legal matters, employment immigration and Consumer issues.

Citizens Advice
Myddelton House
115-123 Pentonville Road
London NI 9LZ
website; www.citizensadvjce org uk

Listening to you

We welcome your comments on how we could improve our service to you. We do this by:

- asking you to fill in comment cards;
- carrying out local surveys;
- paying attention to comments, complaints and suggestions;
- displaying information about our performance;
- displaying details in court Waiting areas of complaints and suggestions we've used to make improvements;
- displaying results of local surveys and changes we plan to make because of them.

If you have a complaint please tell us as soon as possible and we'll do our best to sort out the problem

Barristers

If you'd like a complaint form please write to:
The Complaints Commissioner

General Council of the Bar
Northumberland House
303-306 High Holborn
LondonWClV7iZ
Telephone: 020 7440 4000 or 020 7242 0082
email: ebarilone@barcouncil.org.uk
website: www.barcouncil.org.uk

Compensation

You may be able to claim compensation if you've lost money or run up costs because of a mistake by our staff. You must write to the Court Manager explaining what happened and why you think you should be compensated.

Your letter should include the name of the judge and court, your case number and the hearing date, All letters must include specific details of the conduct about which you are complaining.

Judges don't usually answer letters about cases they've heard. Although we can't look into complaints about solicitors, barristers or any other organisation, you may find this address useful:

Solicitors

The Law Society
Office for the Supervision of Solicitors
Victoria Court
8 Dormer Place

Leamington Spa
Warwickshire CV32 5AE
Helpline: 0845 608 6565
email: enquiries@lawsociety.org.uk
website: www.oss.lawsociety.org.uk

2

COURT CHARTER FOR THE CROWN COURT

This leaflet sets out the standard of service we aim to give you and how you can let us know if you're not happy. We set the standards after talking to people who have used the courts. Most people coming to court will be worried about what to expect. We aim to reduce these worries by giving a good, friendly service. When you come to court you can expect fair and equal treatment, no matter what your race, ethnic origins disability, sex, sexuality or religious beliefs.

If you're coming to court

Before the date of your hearing, you can:

- ask to visit a court room;
- ask us to arrange seats in the court room (if we can) for anyone who comes to your hearing with you. The court building is open from 9am until 5pm and you'll find:
- polite, helpful staff wearing name badges;
- clear signs to help you find your way around;
- information leaflets on display;
- a notice giving the name of our Customer Service Officer who'll be pleased to help you with any special needs, suggestions or complaints.

When you go to the public counter or enquiry point we'll:

- respect your privacy;
- talk to you out of the hearing of other members of the public, if you prefer:

107

- deal with your question within I 0 minutes;
- explain the delay if you have to wait longer.

You can call us between 9am and 5pm and we'll:

- answer the phone quickly and helpfully;
- say who you're speaking to;
- give you a clear and helpful answer.

When you write to the court, and we need to reply, we'll
:

- write to you or phone you within I 0 working days;
- tell you who's writing and tell you how to phone them.

Hearings

We will arrange hearings as quickly as possible. We are trying to reduce delays, but many things can affect how soon we can arrange a trial. Although we can't guarantee when your case will be heard we aim to:

- have the first hearing within 6 weeks from when we get your case (4 weeks if the defendant is in custody);
- start most trials within 16 weeks of when we get the case;
- deal with difficult cases, such as murder or rape trials, within a year.

At the first hearing, the defendant says if they are guilty or not guilty and the judge decides what will happen next.

Being a juror

If we ask you to be a juror we'll:

- send you a jury summons at least 4 weeks before we need you;
- tell you if you could defer or be let off serving as a juror.

We will also send you:

- a booklet (You and Your Jury Service) about your duties plus the expenses and allowances you can claim;
- a map of how to get to court;
- a leaflet with details of public transport and any car parks near the court;
- the times the court is open;
- information on refreshments, telephones, separate waiting areas and so on;
- the name of our Customer Service Officer.

When you arrive at court we'll:

- show you to a separate waiting area;
- show you a video giving you more details about: being a juror;
- make sure one of our staff is available to answer your questions;
- respect your privacy;
- talk to you in private if you prefer;
- tell you how many days you can expect to sit as a juror.

How we use your time

Some people may not be able to sit as jurors on certain trials because, for example, they're connected with the defendant (the accused person) or the case. Also some defendants change their plea to guilty just before the trial is due to start. Because we can't know this, we may have more jurors than we actually need

This means you may not be used as a juror in a trial for every day of your jury service. While you're waiting to sit on a trial we'll:

- use your time as efficiently as possible;
- tell you at least every hour when you're likely to be needed in court;
- let you go as soon as possible if you're not needed.
  We will also:
- let you go back to work on days, or part days, if you aren't needed (if your employer agrees);
- give you a special phone number to call (in our larger Crown Court centres) to find out if you need to come to court that day;

- explain how (in our smaller courts) we make sure you know when you need to come into court.

When you're selected for a jury, you'll have to swear an oath or make an affirmation (promise) when you go into the courtroom. .This requires you to give a true verdict according to the evidence presented during the trial. We will display the words of the most common oaths and the affirmation in the jury waiting area for you to read in advance.

If you're a witness

If your case is delayed you can ask us to:

- explain the delay, or tell you who can explain;
- tell you when your case is likely to be heard.

If we have to change the date of your hearing, we'll let you (or the people who called you as a witness) know as soon as possible.

Waiting at court

You shouldn't have to wait more than 2 hours before you're called to give evidence. But delays can happens for example, if the case before yours takes longer than planned.

If you have to wait we'll:

- tell you regularly how much longer you may have to wait
- tell you as soon as possible, through the people who called you as a witness, if your case can't be heard that day.

We will also:

- provide separate waiting areas in existing courts, if we can;
- make separate waiting areas in new court buildings;
- arrange for you to wait apart from the defendant and the other side's witnesses if there isn't a separate area. Please ask our staff if you'd prefer this.

Our service for child witnesses

We know that giving evidence in court can be very difficult for a child so we'll:

- arrange to have any case involving a child witness heard as soon as possible;
- provide a Child Witness Support Officer or witness Support Officer to make sure everything runs smoothly;
- make sure that someone meets children and their companions when they come to court and takes them to a private waiting area away from the defendant;
- explain how we do things in court and answer any questions.

Sometimes the judge will let a child give evidence using Video Link. If they do, we can arrange for the child to see the room and how the equipment works before the trial. If you want to know whether a Video Link may be used, please ask the lawyers involved in your case.

Witness Service

The Witness Service is run by the independent charity, Victim Supports and helps victims, witnesses and their families before, during and after the hearing. Trained volunteers in every Crown Court centre in England and Wales give free and confidential support and practical information about how we do things in court. They'll normally get in touch with you before the court hearing to offer their help. The help they offer includes:

- arranging a visit to court before the hearing;
- arranging for someone to go into the court room with you if you have to give evidence;
- giving you the chance to talk over the case after it's ended and where to get more help or information.

If you'd like help, or if you'd like to volunteer for the Witness Service, you can contact them at your local Crown Court or write to them at:

Victim Support National Office
Cranmer House
39 Brixton Road
London SW9 6DD
TelephoneO2O 7735 9166

email: contact@victimsupport.org.uk
website: www.victimsupport.org. uk

Travel expenses and allowances

If you're a juror or defence witness you can claim travel expenses and allowances. We will continue to pay jurors expenses and allowances if you sit on a trial we expect to last for more than two working days. If you're a prosecution Witness you should get your claim form from the Crown Prosecution Service. They will:

- explain what expenses and allowances you can claim;

- give you a reply-paid envelope to return your form after you've filled it in.

If you're a Witness, you may be able to claim your expenses and allowances immediately after you've given evidence. We will:

- tell you if you can;
- if you can't, we'll tell you why not.

If you're a defendant found not guilty at your trial, and the judge agrees, you may be able to claim travel expenses and other allowances. But you won't be able to claim for loss of earnings. We will:

- give you a claim form and help you fill it in;
- send you the money within 5 working days from when we get your claim form.

If you are a defendant
If you're on bail, and if you require it, we'll send you or your solicitor:

- a map of how to get to court;
- a leaflet with details of public transport and any car parks near the court;
- the times the court is open;
- information on refreshments, telephone, separate waiting areas and so on;
- the name of our Customer Service Officer.

In many Crown Court centres we have separate waiting areas for defendants who are on bail. If you need an interpreter at court and you don't have a lawyer please let us know as soon as possible. We can arrange an interpreter for you at your hearing. If you can't hear very well and you need help at your court hearing, please speak to our Customer Service Officer who will tell you how we can help you.

We try to arrange hearings as quickly as possible. We're trying to reduce delays, but many things can affect how soon we can arrange trials, so we can't guarantee when your case will be heard.

We do give priority to trials for defendants in custody. If you've been sent for trial from the magistrates court to the Crown Court, we aim to arrange a hearing where you can plead guilty or not guilty:

- if you're in custody, within 4 weeks from when we receive your case;
- if you're on bail, within 6 weeks from when we receive your case.

Appeals

If you're appealing against a decision in the magistrates' court, we will:

- deal with the appeal within 14 weeks of getting it;
- if it takes longer than 14 weeks, we'll tell you the reason for the delay if you ask us. If you've been sent to

the Crown Court from the magistrates' court to be sentenced we aim to sentence you within I 0 weeks from when we receive your case.

At court you'll probably come into contact with people from the police, National Probation Service and Crown Prosecution Service. Although we aren't responsible for the services they provides you can get information about them from the court.

Crown Prosecution Service

This organisation decides if crimes investigated by the police should go to court. If they do, the CPS is responsible for the prosecution case. You can contact them at:

Crown Prosecution Service
50 Ludgate Hill
London EC4M 7EX
Telephone: 020 7735 9166
email: enquires©cps.gsi.gov.uk
website: www.cps.gov.uk

Authorities such as the Inland Revenue and HM Customs and Excise can also bring prosecutions. Please ask our staff for more details.

National Probation Service
National Probation Directorate
Home Office
Horseferry House
Dean Ryle Street

London SWIP2AW
email: npd.publicenquiry@homeoffice.gsi.gov.uk
website: www.homeoffice.gov.uk/justice/probatjon

Legal help
You may be able to get legal help to help pay your legal fees. You can find out by contacting:

The Legal Services Commission
85 Grays Inn Road
London WCIX 8AA
Telephone: 020 7813 1000
email address for regional offices are on their WE
website: www.legalservices.gov.uk

Community Legal Service
The CLS will help you decide the type of legal advice you need.

Telephone: 020 7759 0000
website: www.justask.org.uk

Listening to you
We welcome your comments on how we could improve our service to you. We do this by:

- asking you to fill in comment cards;
- carrying out local surveys;
- paying attention to comments, complaints and suggestions;

- displaying information about our performance;
- displaying details in court waiting areas of complaints and suggestions we've used to make improvements;
- displaying results of local surveys and changes we plan to make because of them. If you have a complaint, please tell us as soon as possible and we'll do our best to sort out the problem there and then. If you're still not happy, you can speak to our Customer Service Officer or Court Manager. If you prefer you can write to the Court Manager of the court in question. If you'd like a complaint form, please ask one of our staff. All complaints will be dealt with quickly and efficiently. We welcome suggestions and compliments too. For more information visit our website at: www.courtservice.gov.uk

We can investigate complaints about how a judge behaved in court but we can't investigate anything to do with their judgment, their assessment of the evidence or any of the decisions they made about the handling of your case. These can only be challenged by way of appeal.

Neither the Department for Constitutional Affairs nor anyone else has the power to investigate or overturn the decisions of the courts and there are no circumstances in which we can consider complaints about judges' decisions. Complaints about the personal conduct of judges should be sent in writing to:

Judicial Correspondence Unit
Department for Constitutional Affairs
PO Box 38528
5th Floor
30 Millbank
London SW I P 4XB
Telephone 020 7217 4840
Fax: 020 7217 4875

Your letter should include the name of the judge and court, your case number and the hearing date. All letters must include specific details of the conduct about which you are complaining. Judges don't usually answer letters about cases they've heard. We can't look into complaints about barristers, solicitors or other organisations but you may find these addresses useful:

Solicitors
The Law Society
Office for the Supervision of Solicitors
Victoria Court
8 Dormer Place
Leamington Spa
Warwickshire CV32 5AE
Helpline: 0845 608 6565
email: enquires@lawsociety.0rg.uk
website:www.oss.iawsociety.org.uk

Barristers

If you'd like a complaint form please write to:

The Complaints Commissioner

General Council of the Bar

Northumberland House

303-306 High Holborn

London WCIV 7jZ

Telephone: 020 7440 4000 or

020 7242 0082

email: ebarilone@barcouncil.org.uk

website: www.barcouncil.0rg.Uk

Police

Police Complaints Authority,

10 Great George Street,

London SWIP 3AE

Telephone: 020 7273 6450

email: Info@pca.gov.uk

website: www.pca.gov.uk

Compensation

You may be able to claim compensation if you've lost money or run up costs because of a mistake by our staff. You must write to the Court Manager explaining what happened and why you think you should be compensated.